D1733726

Developing Charlie

How to Grow Great Employees

Jane Holcomb, Ph.D.

Developing Charlie

Copyright ©1997 by Jane Holcomb, Ph.D.

All rights reserved. No part of this book may be reproduced or utilized in any form or by any means, electronic or mechanical, including photocopying, record-ing, or by any information storage or retrieval system, without permission in writing from the author. Inquiries should be addressed to Jane Holcomb, at ON-Target Training, 7805 West 80th Street, Playa del Rey, CA 90293, or by calling 310-821-7624.

This publication is designed to provide accurate and authoritative information on the subject matter covered. It is sold with the understanding that neither the author nor the publisher is engaged in rendering legal, accounting, or other professional services. If legal advice or other expert assistance is required, the services of a competent professional should be sought.

Credits:

American Media Publishing   Arthur Bauer
    Todd McDonald

Editor in Chief   Karen Massetti Miller
Book Design   Michele Jansen
Illustrations   Jack Linstrom, FAB Artists

Published by American Media Inc.
4900 University Avenue, West Des Moines, IA 50266-6769.

Library of Congress Catalog Card Number 98-070743
Holcomb, Jane, Ph.D.
Developing Charlie

Printed in the United States of America
ISBN 1-884926-79-7

Acknowledgments

Thanks to Keith Tombrink for helping me solidify ideas and for providing a setting where ideas flourish. Thanks to Jim Mackie, who was a model for the manager I describe in the book.

Thanks to Bob Boylan for inspiration, encouragement, and the connection to my illustrator, Jack Linstrom, with FAB Artists in Minneapolis.

Additional thanks to:

- my mentor, George Morrisey
- my colleague, Chris Christenson
- my friend, Sandra Holden
- my model manager, Jim Mackie

for their candid feedback on this book.

Introduction

Developing Charlie was written for managers and supervisors whose job is to develop others in order to accomplish their primary job of delivering quality products and services. They have many employees passing through their lives, and they are responsible for each employee's development during that time. As bosses, they are responsible for hiring, orienting, assigning work, training, coaching, appraising performance, and, finally, saying good-bye. Then, new employees enter their department, and it starts all over again. This book is not about what managers and supervisors should do to improve themselves; it's about *growing great employees.*

The story is told from a manager's point of view and follows three employees through their development from hiring to termination. I have created a fictional manager who will share with you this story and his experience with three new employees as they progress through the organization. The new employees are Chuck, Charleen, and Charles—his three Charlies.

This book is about *Developing Charlie.*

Table of Contents

Chapter 1
Hello, Charlie

- Interviewing Charlie

- Hiring Charlie

- Orienting Charlie

Hello, Charlie

Hi. I'm the manager/supervisor of a mid-sized division of a very large company, Any Company USA, and I want to share a story about three of my employees. The development of these three employees drove home an important lesson for me. As managers or supervisors, we see many employees pass through our lives. As their bosses, we have a profound effect on their lives and the paths their careers take. This awesome responsibility made me pay attention to their growth and development, and to take my role in this never-ending process very seriously. Over the years, I've learned to do some things right, and I hope this story of my three Charlies helps you. It starts several years ago . . .

After downsizing, reengineering, and a hiring freeze in order to rightsize, I'm finally getting the three new employees this department has needed for over a year. They report to me today, and I'm looking forward to some new blood, new faces, new ideas, and a few more hands to get the work done.

They will be here sometime this morning for orientation. Human Resources likes to stagger new hires. They go there first for the typical HR stuff: filling out papers for benefits, getting policy and procedure manuals, and the sermon on absentee rules, sick leave, sexual harassment, and so on.

These three are pretty interesting. I had the final say in selecting them during the hiring process. So, if they turn out to be turkeys, I have no one to blame but myself. There were several applicants for each of these positions. The applications were screened by HR first. Then HR sent the top three or four choices to me for the final decision. After all, I'm the one who has to live with them eight hours a day, five days a week. And I'm the one who will be responsible for their success or failure in this organization.

Interviewing Charlie

When I received the applications from HR, my intention was just to call each candidate for an interview. I thought I'd spend about 15 minutes with each of them, but it wasn't that simple.

Each of the candidates looked good on paper—they must have taken the same resume-writing seminar because it was hard to tell the difference at first glance. So I needed to do a little homework. We haven't hired anyone in so long that I lost my intuitive knack for it.

First, I went back to review the job descriptions for each position. What were these people expected to do? I know what the jobs are really like, so I had to think of the knowledge, skills, and attitudes necessary to make someone successful in this organization. I thought of some people who are successful and remembered those who have been successful in the past. What were they like? What kind of attitude did they need to fit the job and work well here? How much knowledge did they need going in, and what did they learn on the job? How smart, how educated, how personable must they be to succeed?

One thing I've learned from years of management: Turnover is expensive. It's also an emotional strain to put your hopes, time, and energy into developing employees only to see them fail. When this happens, I think I should have seen the writing on the wall. I ask myself what indicators could have told me about someone who couldn't cut it. So now I'm much more cautious about each step in the hiring process. It's sure easier to pick the right employees the first time than it is to train them and lose them.

I interviewed them carefully, too. I've learned not to trust my memory. Now I take time before each interview to review the job description, my expectations, and the candidate's application and resume. I even call references and ask a few revealing questions. I found if they liked the person and were sorry to lose him or her, they were quick to tell me good things about them. They are interested in their former coworker and say things like, "Say hi to Charlie for me."

If the person was a problem, a troublemaker, or got fired, the people you call are closemouthed. They only give you rank and serial number, or, in this case, dates of employment and positions held. Some organizations have trained their managers and supervisors on what they may and may not say in response to calls such as mine. But I still find their responses revealing.

Once I called an employee's reference to find it was a relative who was caught off guard by my call. This told me a lot about the candidate, whom I ended up not interviewing. I save my face-to-face interview time for only those I think will be a good match for me and this organization. If something suspicious turns up before the interview, like someone lying about education or prior salary, I'm wasting my time with an interview.

Did you know that according to a study done by Adler in *Winning the Hiring Game,* 34 percent of candidates falsify job applications? I guess applicants think no one will check, and frankly, most of the time they don't. I never used to; now I do.

Before we downsized, these people would have reported to supervisors, who would have been included in the interview process. We would discuss qualifications in advance, and their supervisors would have the final say. Now, with our flatter organization, Charles and Chuck report directly to me.

We asked Charleen's department leader to participate in the selection process, but she had a crisis at the time and said, "Find a warm body—anyone could do the job." So, I interviewed several people. I knew what I wanted to ask them and what I wanted to tell them about our organization and about me.

You have to be careful, because there are many things you might want to know but can't ask. For example, questions on the following topics are *not* allowed:

- Nationality or origin

- Pregnancy or family plans

- Age, height, weight

- Education—only if relevant for the job is it okay to inquire about it

- Physical impairments

- Race (no photo may be required)

- Religion

- Arrests or previous criminal records

All of this has to do with issues of discrimination. I understand the reason for it, but if a manager isn't trained and aware, there could be problems.

I interview candidates in our lunchroom. I believe they're more comfortable and at ease there than in my office. I want them to be relaxed and talk freely. I remember how stressful job interviews were when I was young and anxious. So I offer them a cup of coffee, and we talk informally for a while. I tell them about tasks they would perform, what a typical day is like, and about the culture of the organization. I tell them my expectations and answer questions they might have. I ask some questions about their background and experience, based mostly on things mentioned in their resumes. I also inquire about problems they faced and solved on previous jobs.

Some questions I like to ask include:

- What did you do in your previous job?

- How would you handle this problem . . . ?

- Why do you think you would like this job?

- When I call your references, what will they tell me?

Sometimes, I actually give people an impromptu skills test. I was hiring for a routine production-line job that required someone who could focus on the same task for several hours and who had good eye-hand coordination. Someone who is quick and well coordinated can produce twice as much at this type of job than someone who is uncoordinated and moves slowly. I had this little skills test I gave to everyone—just a simple puzzle. I asked them to put it together as fast as they could. I could tell by watching them if they had a good eye and quick fingers.

I generally take applicants on the floor to check out the work environment. I try to give them a realistic picture of what their lives will be like here. I tell them the good news and the bad news while asking if they think they can handle it—and if they can picture themselves doing this job. I get to know them best during these informal tours.

We get acquainted, and when we're done, I let them know what will happen next and when to expect to hear from us. I thank them for their time without letting them think they have the job just because the interview went well. I believe it's very important to call unsuccessful candidates as soon as the decision is made, so they can look elsewhere for a job.

When a candidate leaves, I take time to document and evaluate that candidate before the next one arrives. I've created a checklist so I can rate each person using the same criteria. It helps justify my recommendation to HR and to those we did not hire.

A sample of my checklist is on the next page. It's pretty simple—just a memory jogger. I rate applicants in the same way a teacher completes a school report card: A, B, C, D, or F. Numbers would work too: 5–1, for example, with 5 being highest and 1 the lowest. You could also use a few words to jog your memory. I put additional personal thoughts on the bottom of my checklist.

I get a feeling for what candidates *can* do from their knowledge, skills, experience, and education. I get a sense of what they *will* do from their attitude, energy, motivation, and goals. I think I did a good job hiring these three, but only time will tell.

Steps in the Interview Process

Before the Interview

- Human Resources receives and screens applications
- Manager or the team receives eligible applications and resumes
- Manager and/or the team reviews job description for knowledge, skills, and attitudes needed to be successful
- Someone checks references to get a sense of the candidate and to make sure statements are accurate

During the Interview

- Create a relaxed environment
- Ask about their experience and qualifications and tell them about the organization
- Use an interview guide to keep track of each candidate
- End the interview with clear information about what happens next

After the Interview

- Review qualifications of each candidate
- Discuss the information with others who might supervise or work with him or her
- Let the rejected candidates know as soon as possible so they can look elsewhere

Interview Guide

Name _____

Experience				
Education				
Knowledge				
Skills				
Attitude				
Problem Solving				
Team Experience				
Communication Skills				

Comments:

* You can use numbers, letters, or symbols to evaluate the candidate. This is a memory system for you. Some candidates have several interviews or are interviewed by several different people. Make sure each person who evaluates uses the same system.

Hiring Charlie

So, who are these characters? We hired Chuck for outside sales, Charleen for a routine shipping and mail room job, and Charles for setting up information systems.

Chuck, now he's a real winner. Young, good looking, bright, and high energy. His gregarious, friendly attitude will go a long way to win customers. He's the type who makes you smile even when you're angry or upset. Chuck graduated from college and has spent two years in the Coast Guard. He has no family commitments, so he can travel. He worked in retail sales while in college, in a popular clothing store, a national chain. He looks sharp, dresses like an ad in a magazine—conservative, but in the latest fashion. Drives a sporty little car. Chuck thinks the world is his oyster, and I guess it is. He seemed eager to get started, but impatient, as if he had another appointment waiting.

Chuck's job here will be outside sales. He will deal directly with our customers: building relationships, consulting, teaching them about our products and services, and trouble-shooting when problems arise. I think his outgoing, friendly personality is perfect for this position. Communication skills are his strong suit, and that's what we need.

Charleen is a quiet single mother who was willing to do anything we had available. She really needed the job, and we needed someone to do routine shipping and mailing work. Charleen volunteered a lot about herself in our interview. She is recently divorced, has a couple of young kids and a mother who will baby-sit. She is striking out on her own, like it or not. She seems young, without much education; but it's not relevant for this job, so I didn't ask. She's a shy, soft-spoken woman, and she should have no problem getting along with our internal customers. I hope they don't cause her too much grief, because she seems kind of frail.

Charleen's job here will be to follow directions from the department manager and assist in mailing products and information to those who need it. Nobody will ask her to make many decisions, so the job won't cause much stress. She seems to want something without challenge anyway. Just tell her what to do, and in her own quiet way she'll get it done. Charleen is the type who causes no trouble . . . and may be overlooked if you're not careful.

Then there's Charles. He's one of those young, arrogant computer whiz kids. Based on our organization's strategic plans, I know I'll need his skills to meet our goals. But the guy has an inflated ego—oh well, maybe it's just youth. He's super bright, an academic egghead who uses a lot of computer jargon no one understands. He was reading one of those computer magazines while he was waiting for our interview. He notices everything and asked a lot of questions about our current computer system.

His job, of course, will be to update our system and create programs we can use internally for tracking and monitoring our production, sales, and other operations. Every department contributed to the wish list of things for Charles to do. He didn't seem turned off by the amount of work; in fact, he seemed to get excited in a low-key way about the challenge and our promise to get him the technical resources he would need. I might find it a little difficult to have someone who sees himself as "the smartest guy in the world" working for me. But I'll help him shape up!

Orienting Charlie

Well, here they come for orientation. Ordinarily, we do orientation individually. But ordinarily, we hire individually too. I'm a firm believer in personally spending time with each new employee in my group to make sure a new employee gets off to a good start. I remember my first hour, day, and week on the job—and it was a nightmare. No one seemed to expect me; there was no work for me to do and nobody to show me around.

As soon as I became a manager, I vowed not to do that myself. Now, I personally greet new employees and spend the first hour showing them around, answering questions, and trying to make them feel like part of the team. This is my time to communicate my high expectations of them and give them an overall look at the facility, the job, and especially their workstations.

I take them around and introduce them to coworkers, other managers they might need to know, team leaders and supervisors they will work with. I explain some of the unwritten rules that exist in every organization and generally tell them what's expected of them to be successful.

One of my better ideas was the buddy system. All new employees are assigned a buddy to work with. It's usually the person hired just before them, the newest hire. Someone who has been here long enough to know the organization, and new enough to remember what it was like to be the new kid on the block. The buddy answers questions people don't want to ask their bosses—questions like, "Where's the copy machine?" Buddies show new hires local places to have lunch, and encourage them to join the company softball team . . . or whatever goes on after work. I guess I get a little carried away with my motivational speech. I call it encouragement—employees call it the boss's new hire sermon. Then, I turn the new hires over to their direct supervisors, if they have one; sometimes it's a team leader, who will give them details of the job, what they're accountable for, standards, goals, and so on.

Surveys from exit interviews show most people who leave, even after a year or more, say they never felt like part of the organization. They always felt like outsiders. Part of making them feel included is being sure they have meaningful work to do from the start. The orientation is a process for making them feel like one of the family. By doing the orientation myself, I get to know these people better. They seem to loosen up after they have been hired. This helps me understand their experience, their attitude, and especially their self-confidence. Let me tell you what happened during orientation with my three Charlies. I use an Orientation Guideline to make sure I cover everything while we tour the facility and get acquainted.

Charleen was the first to come in. This is not a formal place, and she'll work in the mail room. But she had no idea that jeans, a tee shirt, and tennis shoes are not proper working attire. Charleen will have a supervisor to whom she reports, so some of her development will come from that source. I guess when you're a young mother at home raising two small children, that's how you would dress. It's hard to convey to young people how important their appearance is. Like it or not, we judge people at first by what we see. Charleen's appearance labels her as a young, unsophisticated, blue-collar, behind-the-scenes worker. Her demeanor tells me she's overwhelmed and scared to death about coming to work. She has no confidence in her skills or ability to learn the job.

I oriented Charleen by showing her around the facility, telling her where to find things and letting her know this is a friendly place to work. I emphasized she would soon feel at home and said she could call me any time. I took her to my office to show her where I live and then introduced her to her supervisor. Her supervisor assigned a buddy who would show her the ropes and have lunch with her the first day. She got a locker to store her personal things. I had a little time, so I stayed while the supervisor walked her around the mail room and explained what others were doing. The supervisor and her new buddy took a short break to talk with Charleen, have coffee, and make her feel welcome. I left feeling she was in good hands. Charleen thanked me profusely for giving her a job and an opportunity. I know she'll do her best here.

My next orientation was with Charles. I can't believe he arrived late for his first day on the job. He explained he was working on a new computer program and lost track of time. As we walked through the facility, he was mildly interested in meeting other people, but highly interested in their technology. He asked lots of questions about the machinery and how it operated, never hesitating to comment on existing newer technology. It's a little annoying, but that's why I hired him. He has knowledge and skills in the area we need to move into.

His interest peaked when I showed him his office—rather his cubicle. He immediately sat in his chair and turned on his computer. He had several questions about where he could get information, manuals, and directories. He also asked about budgets for new equipment and software. Funny, he asked if he could bring in his own chair—I guess the one we have doesn't suit him. I found someone from accounting who volunteered to be his buddy. When they were introduced, Charles didn't seem very interested . . . as if this person was an intrusion. Charles is a funny guy: He's extremely confident about his technical skill and thinks that's all he needs. I hope I can make him see it takes more than technical skill to function well in an organization like ours. He seems to think we're fortunate to have him . . . instead of him being fortunate to have a job.

Chuck was the last of the three to go through orientation. He arrived exactly at the agreed time, not a minute early. He looked sharp: suit, tie, and all smiles. As we walked through the facility, he wanted to meet everyone, grinned, shook hands, and asked lots of questions. He seems interested in knowing each person and learning who does what and who reports to whom. He actually had a note pad and took notes now and then.

When I took him to his office, the first thing he wanted to know was how to use the phone system. Then he wanted to meet our receptionist, who runs the switchboard. We talked a while about the products and services he'll sell and about current clients. He wanted to know everything I knew about our clients—especially the major accounts assigned to him. He asked some client questions I couldn't answer, and I've dealt with these clients for years. I called in another salesperson who will be Chuck's buddy. They started talking about clients, and before I knew it there were three others in the room laughing, joking, and getting to know Chuck. Since it was almost lunch-time, I invited the others to join us; we went to a new, local, popular restaurant. Chuck has made some friends and seems quite comfortable in our environment.

My Orientation Guide reminds me to cover things I think these new employees need to know about the organization. When you've done this many times, you tend to forget a few things you've come to take for granted, but those things are still important information for new employees.

Orientation Guide

- **About the company**
  Products
  Markets
  Organizational structure
  Policies and procedures
  Culture
  Key management personnel
  Facilities
  Unwritten rules for getting along

- **About the job**
  What, when, how, why, where

- **About accountability**
  Responsibilities
  Authority
  Priorities

- **About performance standards and goals**

- **About working with other groups**
  Nature of the groups
  Good relations
  Best coordination
  Appropriate schedules

- **About the workplace and the employee's workstation**

Summary—Hello, Charlie
Key Points

- Think about hiring people you want to work with every day.

- Read resumes carefully, and check references—you will learn some interesting things.

- Turnover is expensive—and an emotional strain.

- Don't trust your memory; write comments after each interview.

- Let supervisors who must train the new hires help select them.

- Educate yourself on what you may and may not ask applicants.

- Give applicants the good news and the bad news about the job.

- Be professional and considerate by letting the unsuccessful applicants know your decision as soon as possible.

- Orientation is very important:
    1) Make your new hires feel important by being there to greet them on their first day.
    2) Have some meaningful work for them to do.
    3) Arrange for a buddy to answer questions and take them to lunch.

- Create an Orientation Guide so all the bases are covered no matter who does the orientation.

Chapter 2

Assigning Work

- Who Is Charlie?

- Identifying and
  Clarifying Expectations

- Setting Goals and
  Performance Standards

Who Is Charlie?

Well, now that I have these three new employees, it's time to put them to work. One of the things I tried to pay attention to when I was hiring them was to look for personalities that matched the jobs. Taking a little time to consider who they are also helps with communication on all levels. Let me show you how it works.

We have basic behavioral styles that form our personalities and follow us everywhere . . . except for a few Jekyll-and-Hyde characters who are totally different at work than they are everywhere else. For the most part, according to Carl Jung, a psychologist who studied personalities ages ago, there are four basic personality types. I call them Controllers, Promoters, Supporters, Analyzers. If you can determine your style of communication, then determine the style of your employees, you will have some insight on how best to deal with them.

Let's take a look at my behavioral style and then my three new employees. I'm what you call a Controller. That means I like to run the show, make decisions, and tell others what to do. I'm very direct, to the point, and down to business. I have no time to waste. So, if you want my attention and respect, get something accomplished. I appreciate others who are assertive, know their jobs, show up on time, and get things done.

Sometimes I am accused of being bossy, aggressive, and insensitive. I've really had to train myself to back off and empower others to do what would take me less time to do myself. So, I try to coach when I can and stay out of the way. I never forget, however, that the success of this division is my responsibility, and I intend to get results. Enough about me; let's talk about my new employees.

I'll start with Chuck. His personality style is the Promoter. He's outgoing, friendly, energetic, and enthusiastic. These are the very qualities that make him a good match for our field position. He will be able to charm the toughest customer with the hardest problems. His engaging smile makes it impossible to stay angry at him. He has one of those bounce-back personalities. Rejections get him down for a bit, but then he's right back up again. I wish more people had his positive, optimistic attitude. Here's a guy who thinks life is a bowl of cherries, and he was put here to have fun.

Sounds great, but I know I'm going to have a few problems with this young man. First of all, he's unorganized: If not disciplined, he'll go off enthusiastically on a tangent and, before he's done, he's on to something else. He's very emotional and tends to exaggerate. He can generate lots of creative ideas but isn't good at sorting out the details. His good qualities far outweigh these problems, and I know he will be successful here.

Charleen, on the other hand, is a Supporter—she's anything but flashy. In fact, she is so quiet and cooperative that she tends to go unnoticed. She will open up and talk in a one-on-one conversation, but she rarely shares her ideas in groups and almost never tries to push them on others. She works well with others and has already bonded with some of the other women in her department

Charleen is not a fighter. She is a shy, sensitive person who will avoid conflict at all costs. She is thoughtful, giving, helpful —always there when someone needs a helping hand. Her supervisor's job will be to bring her out a little—give her a little more confidence and encouragement. I must remember to give her a few additional pats on the back. Self-starters like me don't need that, so I tend to forget people like Charleen do. I know one thing: If I can gain her trust and loyalty, I'll have a dedicated worker and friend for life.

And then there's Charles, your typical Analyzer. He's hard for me to deal with, but I respect his brains and abilities. Charles is my detail person. He is precise; has facts and figures to back up his decisions; operates in a logical, systematic fashion; and makes few mistakes. He is well organized and works well alone. He creates his own projects and enjoys the challenges others consider problems.

Charles is slow to make a decision because he analyzes every aspect of it. But he'll come up with the right solution through careful, systematic problem solving. I enjoy his company because he is always into some project and thinks on a different level than everyone else—not more creative, just more in-depth.

He has a very dry sense of humor in a quiet way: You must listen to catch his jokes. He's quite clever, actually. The problem with Charles is that he can be very stubborn. He thinks his way is the right way, and there is only one right way. He's pretty inflexible. He gets stressed out under pressure and tight deadlines. As long as he has plenty of time to work things out, he's fine. Now if I can keep that arrogant ego of his under control, he might make it around here.

Identifying and Clarifying Expectations

To get my new hires started, or whenever I assign someone to a new task, I start with a Work Plan. My Work Plan is like a laundry list. It works for a variety of tasks and gives me a place to start. Here are some things on my Work Plan:

- **What needs to be done and why.** I believe employees are more willing to do tasks as I describe them if they know the reason we do it that way. I used to just tell people what to do. When they took shortcuts and did things incorrectly, like ignoring safety procedures or turning in incomplete paperwork, it was generally because they didn't understand the need. Sometimes they come up with a creative way to improve the process, which is fine. I like that, provided they clearly understand what needs to be done—and why.

- **What comes first.** Generally, there are steps or a best sequence for doing tasks. Sometimes it's important to do the steps in order, and sometimes it's important just to make sure all of the steps are complete. I like to give employees lots of leeway on how to do things.

  However, I realize they need a lot of direction at first—especially Charleen. She wants someone to tell her exactly how to do something, and she will do it just that way.

Work Plan

TASKS	STANDARDS	GOALS	MEASUREMENT

- Tasks—listed daily or weekly and prioritized
- Standards—what's typically achieved for that task
- Goals—changes according to experience, external factors, etc.
- Measurement—how the task will be evaluated, number of items, number of errors, number completed, etc.

Now take Chuck. You show him how to do something, and he immediately thinks of some creative way to get it done. If it gets done, that is. Making him do it my way would bore and smother him; he wants to do it a new way each time. I must learn to step back and empower them to do what they need to do. Sometimes I put too much importance on my sequence, that is, on doing the steps in the order that makes best sense to me. I'm getting better at focusing on results. As long as the job gets done on time, I'm happy.

- **Use job aids.** Over time we have created job aids to help people with their work. Job aids become a resource tool for employees. Actually, some of the employees have created their own job aids and shared their ideas with teammates. Some of those ideas have become standard procedures in my department. Now I use some of the job aids whenever assigning work.

  Some job aids are just checklists or charts. Others are steps for operating a machine that have been laminated and attached to the machine. The checklist I use for assigning work is my personal job aid. I'm hoping Charles, with his computer skills and ability to create graphics, will help us create some new job aids. We've had some good ideas come up in team meetings but have not had the skill to produce them.

Setting Goals and Performance Standards

Set goals and performance standards for each task. I like to start employees off by breaking their jobs down into smaller tasks. I'll give them three or four tasks to start with. Each task will have a standard of performance and some expectations for reaching the standard. I explain that standards stay the same, but goals change. Their goals can reach and exceed what is standard. There's an old saying we use about SMART goals: They are specific, measurable, achievable, relevant, and timely. Now I fully realize expectations for reaching standards vary with an employee's experience, expertise, and personality style. Charles, for example, will reach performance standards very quickly. He is probably already capable of doing what we expect and then some. On the other hand, Charleen will take a while to meet standards. This is essentially her first job, and everything is new to her.

My expectations for reaching our performance standards are very different for these three employees. Nevertheless, it's important to break the job down into tasks with a standard or goal for each task. I generally take this one step further and also tell them exactly how I will evaluate their success in accomplishing the task. It's important for them to know the methods I use to evaluate them. It creates a common language for us to use when I coach them later, and finally when I write performance appraisals.

At first, I don't expect them to achieve the standard. My expectations for my employees are that they will eventually each pass the standard and set their own goals. We'll fill out a Work Plan together.

Problems, problems, problems. Every job has problems, barriers, challenges; these are what make it a job. We hire employees to deal with these problems. If there were no problems, we could have robots doing the work. Over the years, I've come to know which problems are in various jobs. Without exaggerating them, I try to prepare my people for problems they might encounter. I also share ideas on how to troubleshoot or deal with some of the problems. What I recommend for anticipating problems is Plan B.

If something goes wrong, be prepared with a contingency plan. Think about Plan B in advance—not during a crisis mode. For example, Charles might run into technical problems with our computer systems; it has happened before. Once, our entire system was down for two days. It reminds us of how dependent we've become on computers and their programs. He will also have problems getting money if he wants highfalutin equipment that only he understands. He'll have to temper his "techie talk" to sell his needs to upper management. Chuck, on the other hand, won't need much in the way of resources. But he will have some problems, even difficult customers to deal with. I can alert him to some of their past problems and clue him in on who might present future problems.

Customers seem to fall under the 80/20 rule: 20 percent of your customers cause 80 percent of your problems, and 80 percent of your sales come from 20 percent of your customers. If I can help Chuck identify the 20 percent, it will help him focus his energy where it will be most productive. So that's my guideline for assigning work:

- What needs to be done and why

- Steps or sequence of events

- Job aids and resources

- Set goals and performance standards

- Problem alert

Employees need to know you have high expectations for them and that you think they can do the tasks and do them well. They need to know you're there to support and monitor their progress. We give employees all kinds of subtle verbal and nonverbal feedback regarding our expectations of their performance. They are not stupid—and even if they're young, uneducated, or from another country, they quickly catch on to what you expect. So, if you want them to succeed, keep reinforcing your high expectations of their performance.

One more thing. Every organization has unwritten rules that contribute to an employee's success. When assigning work, it helps to discuss some of these things: ethical issues, getting along with team members, who needs to be informed of what, who are the informal leaders, who to go to for help, and other things that may help your new hire succeed.

Summary—Assigning Work
Key Points

- Try to match personalities and jobs; everyone will be happier and more successful with a good match.

- Learn about behavioral styles and how to work with them.

- Make your expectations crystal clear.

- Use job aids as much as possible to help employees remember.

- Describe the standard for a task (this task should be done in 10 minutes, or you should do 20 of these in an hour).

- Set a goal that's appropriate for each employee to achieve.

- Let your employees know about past and potential problems related to their jobs.

- Help employees create backup plans.

- Tell employees about the "unwritten rules" that could determine success or failure.

- Managers generally get what they expect—have high expectations for your employees.

Chapter 3

Training Charlie

- Performance Management

- On-the-Job Training

- Providing Support

Performance Management

Now that I've put these people to work and know a little about their abilities, it's time to train them. Training will occur as a result of assessing their performance. Most of their training will be on the job. My focus is on improving performance, and I'll use any intervention available to accomplish the task. After all, their performance affects my productivity and helps me meet my goals.

I recently took a class on training employees and learned a new way of thinking. Training is not limited to traditional classroom training or on-the-job training. It's about performance improvement, which means doing whatever it takes to help employees improve their performance and be more productive.

On-the-job training follows these four basic steps: Tell them, show them, let them do it, give them feedback on results. When it comes to other kinds of training such as leadership, communication skills, decision making, etc., performance management is more appropriate.

Performance management takes a broader view, looking for the cause of the problem and the most appropriate, cost-effective intervention, which might not be traditional training. At one time, training implied classroom sessions. Those sessions are still used, but they're not the only way to train. Technology, global multiple locations, and tight budgets have changed all that. In my role of developing my employees, I'm now a performance-improvement manager.

Performance improvement has these four phases:

- **Needs Assessment:** Look at the gap between what is and what should be, and ask questions about what is causing the gap.

- **Possible Interventions:** Consider what we could possibly do to help the employee close the gap. This could include formal training sessions, on-the-job training, or something suggested by the manager, team, or employee.

- **Implementation Plan:** Created with employees for their development based on what the employee needs, the team needs, the organization needs. The plan helps the employee merge personal goals with organizational goals.

- **Evaluation of Results:** Can take many forms and address many levels. Employees can evaluate their own progress with action plans, checklists, or career plans. I evaluate results of their development at performance-appraisal time and in periodic coaching sessions.

ASTD Performance Management Model

Performance
Analysis

- What is?—What should be?
- Is gap in performance consistent or situational?
- What is the impact of the gap?

Cause
Analysis

- Why does the gap exist?
- Importance of consequences, rewards, expectations, resources, feedback, barriers, motivation, knowledge, skills

Interventions

- Possible ways to close the gap

Implementation

- Address the causes
- Clarify the need for the intervention
- Have a clear sense of desired outcome with Action Plan to support it

Change
Management

- Monitor the intervention
- Measure change and collect data

Evaluation

- Results achieved
- Lessons learned
- Recommendations

* ASTD Models for Human Performance Improvement, William Rothwell, 1996

Let's look at the different needs of my three Charlies. Take Chuck, who must acquire lots of knowledge to do his job. He has to learn about our products and services. He has to learn his territory and his customers, their current uses, and their future needs. He must acquire most of this on his own. I can give him product manuals and some hands-on demonstrations. I can give him maps and customer history files. I can go on some sales calls with him to introduce him to new accounts, but most of this knowledge he has to learn on his own time and through his own effort. Occasionally, we send new salespeople to external sales training classes if they request them. As their performance-improvement manager, I'll do whatever it takes to help them succeed.

On the other hand, Charleen has skills that must be developed. She can be trained in a classroom on safety procedures. We have safety meetings monthly. She must learn how to operate equipment, fill out forms, find things. It will take time to get acquainted with how we do things in shipping, mailing, and inventory. I expect her skills to improve at a steady pace. Her buddy will help her; so will her supervisor. We've developed several job aids over the years in her department that should help her. We have checklists posted and color coding for most items. Our shipping software has been customized for us, and the manuals were redone to be user friendly. It might take a little more time for Charleen since she has little formal education and lacks experience.

Then there is Charles. As you know, his knowledge and skills already exceed everyone else's when it comes to computers and various software programs. He'll have to find his own sources of training if he needs technical information. Some of his training should focus on attitude. We have some in-house classes on team building and communication skills that might help. He needs to learn the value of working well with other people to get what you want and get the job done. Up to now, he has made it by being a Lone Ranger. This attitude won't work well here. Charles needs an attitude adjustment to improve his performance with his coworkers. Possible interventions: some coaching from me, classes on being a good communicator and becoming a good listener. Also, feedback sessions with peers, and perhaps a feedback session with a consultant. Evaluating the results of his training will ultimately be done by peers and those he needs to work with in other departments.

Here's an important concept that I want all of my employees to understand: They are always in training—and so am I. We all have to maintain the attitude that training and learning never end. Not only to keep up with changes, and there are plenty of them around here, but to continually improve performance, raise goals, and grow as individuals. There's no guarantee about job stability, so the more employees can improve their skills, the more they'll be worth on their next job. And I mean improve knowledge, skills, and attitude. It's my job to manage their performance improvement.

There are some basic principles I learned in the training class on working with and teaching adults. There are others, but I keep these principles in mind when I have to train employees; they're the ones that really stick, the ones I can use.

- People have different needs and learn at different rates. Some are quick, some are slow, but they can all learn if you use a little patience.

- They come in here with past experience, so if I can link what they need to know to something they already know, it makes learning easier for them.

- Adults want to know how what they learn can be applied to their job or to help them solve problems. They want information they can use, and they want it in logical steps.

Things That Help Adults Learn

- High expectations

- Proper preparation before the learning event

- Lessons prepared for each learning style

    - the visual learner
    - the audio learner
    - the kinesthetic learner
      (the one who must touch and feel)

- Job aids: charts, graphs, pictures, cue cards, etc.

- Invite questions by asking, "What questions do you have?"
  rather than asking, "Are there any questions?"

- Information on how their learning will be evaluated or measured

- Follow up to identify problems in transfer

- Reward for those who use new skills well

    and...

- Confidence they can learn—with a little patience

- Linking new information to what they already know

- Applying new information to current problems

On-the-Job Training

On-the-job training, the kind done one-on-one for developing a skill or with a group performing a task, hasn't changed much since my old training days. This generally means they all need to do the same thing the same way. It goes like this: After you assign work, break it down into smaller tasks and see how they do.

- Tell them
- Show them
- Provide practice
- Give them feedback

Tell them. When you tell them what the task involves, use visuals, such as training manuals, pictures, charts, and graphs. We're using videos now, and computers, to help people understand how to do their jobs.

Give employees information in a positive way. For example, if I say, "Don't think of a pink elephant on roller skates with a blue hat on," what immediately pops into your mind? At some point, the "dos and don'ts" get mixed up, and it's hard to remember which is which. Focus on telling employees what you want them to remember. Tell them about the big picture and how their jobs fit into company goals.

Show them. When you show them what to do, you are demonstrating how you would do it. Sometimes I can do the task myself, so I'll show them how I do it. Most of the time, I let someone else show them, someone who does the job daily. New employees are more likely to ask other employees questions rather than their supervisor or manager. You have to be careful though: Experienced employees have picked up shortcuts or their own ways of doing things. The people who show new employees what to do must do it right themselves. Nothing makes employees angrier than when they are dinged for doing something wrong—when that's how someone else trained them.

How will I show my three Charlies what to do? For Chuck, it might mean showing him how we keep track of sales records and write purchase orders. All salespeople do it the same for consistency and accounting. For Charleen, it means finding a willing and able employee to show her manuals, directories, job aids, and how things work in her department. For Charles, it means showing him how each department uses its technology now and letting him help the department upgrade its programs. I'm concerned that his attitude might keep him from getting cooperation from those he needs to work with.

Provide practice. Some things can be practiced on the spot, in a training class, or on the job. Some things take time. For example, I took a class on how to conduct effective staff meetings, and my next official staff meeting was in six weeks. I couldn't practice a real staff meeting until then, and a lot of what I learned was lost. I need to make sure my employees have an opportunity to practice and get feedback on their training right away. Each of my employees needs a different kind of support from me.

I could practice some telephone sales calls with Chuck or monitor a few of his calls to make sure he knows the basics. I'll introduce him to a few customers, watch how he works with them; and see how he presents our products and services. You know, a little hand-holding to set him on the right foot until he feels confident. Charleen will have to practice using our inventory software on her own. Her buddy can be there to answer questions and help her learn the system. As she gets experience and practice, her skill will improve. I'll check on her progress now and then and ask her buddy how she's doing.

Charles will have to practice being less of a know-it-all and more aware of what others offer. He has to practice being in the helping mode, which means asking for input from others. I think I'll recommend training in active listening and encourage him to practice those skills. This will take some follow-up on my part, which leads to my next point.

Give them feedback. I'll have to give Charles plenty of feedback on how he's doing. Actually, they all need lots of feedback while being trained, not only to let them know how they're doing, but to reinforce and encourage. Feedback should be positive, specific, and focus on improvement. Remember the self-fulfilling prophecy about communicating high expectations? Well, it especially applies to training, when employees are feeling uncomfortable about learning something new.

Productivity experts say the best environment for learning is 75/25. Seventy-five percent of the time the learners are getting positive feedback and reinforcement. Twenty-five percent of the time they're being corrected or told they did it wrong. On a good day, I manage 50/50. What was it like when you were being trained? Probably the reverse of the ideal.

Providing Support

There are three things I can do as a manager to support any training effort that takes place with my employees. I can coach and counsel before training, address environmental barriers, and follow up by rewarding and reinforcing success.

First, I can coach and counsel them before training. Doing so will let them know why they're being trained, how this training will help them on the job, and what I expect to see when they return. We need to agree on a follow-up. Perhaps there will be a discussion on what they learned; perhaps it's something to report at a staff meeting; perhaps a demonstration. For example, Charles might learn some things in a team-building class, and we might just talk about how they apply | to him and his team. Chuck might get an update on some of our customers, their problems, and their future plans and present it at a staff meeting. And Charleen—well, I could take a few minutes, go down to shipping, and let her show me how well she's doing.

When employees know in advance that someone will evaluate or follow-up on their training, somehow it affects the attitude they bring into the learning situation. They have more of a heads-up, pay-attention attitude because someone will ask about this later.

Second, during training and the transition period that follows, trainees run into barriers that can sabotage the training effort. There are some things I can do to keep this from happening. Trainers and trainees can't be expected to maintain their regular workload during training. Interrupting training sessions with phone calls and daily problems is a sure way to create a barrier. Training takes a person's full attention, and interruptions are distractions that can sabotage.

The best training is provided when the employee needs it; just-in-time training is the most effective. I remember thinking, why didn't they give me supervisory training when I was promoted instead of several months later? Why didn't we provide customer-service training before we lost some customers, instead of as a result of complaints? Why didn't we train people on the new computer program when they could use it, instead of six months before it was installed? By the time they needed it, their new skills were forgotten, and the time and money spent on ill-timed training was wasted.

Training should be considered part of the culture, part of the job—not a punishment for nonperformance or a reward that equals a day off work. Training should be fun, challenging, interactive, timely, relevant, and interesting. It can be all of this and still improve a trainee's knowledge, skills, and attitudes. So it's up to me to provide training—good training that will meet my objectives to improve performance and be fun and interesting for my employees.

Third, after training, follow up with rewards and reinforcement. It's the part most related to whether or not learning will transfer from the classroom to the work site or from on-the-job training to continual improvement. What kind of support and reinforcement are given to the trainee when the training session is complete? Providing an environment that will encourage my trainees to blossom is my job. So I pay a lot of attention to them when training sessions are finished.

I try to find creative ways to reward trainees. They love certificates, celebrations, awards, and such. But the biggest impact comes from my evaluation of their progress, which I try to relate to training and always mention on performance appraisals. Promotions based on certain training, as a prerequisite, help reinforce the value placed on training by the organization. So it's my job to support classroom training, on-the-job training, self-directed learning, college courses, any and all training. I do this by coaching employees before training, addressing barriers that might interfere during training, and providing rewards and reinforcements afterwards. It sounds like one more responsibility added to my overloaded agenda. But if growing great employees is my responsibility, then so is supporting their training and development.

Summary—Training Charlie
Key Points

- Think "performance management"—look for many interventions to improve your employees' performance.

- Create a learning organization by encouraging all employees to develop their knowledge and skills.

- Timing is important—train employees when they need to learn.

- Confucius said, "I hear, I forget. I see, I remember. I do, I learn."

- Be sure your trainer is a good role model.

- Practice—Practice—Practice

- Provide your support for training by coaching employees before the training, addressing environmental barriers during transition, and rewarding and reinforcing new skills after training.

- All training must be directly related to the job

Chapter 4

Coaching Charlie

- Using Active Listening

- Giving Feedback

- Problem-Solving Steps

Coaching Charlie

So, now I'm a coach. I used to coach Little League; now I coach employees. I have a plaque in my office that says, "Coaching is multiple interventions given at appropriate times to unlock potential and improve performance."

My definition of coaching is, "Anything that will make them successful and productive." Coaching never ends, unlike performance appraisals that take place once a year, or formal coaching sessions ideally planned with quarterly meetings. Real coaching takes place daily.

Here are my thoughts on coaching, and on a big mistake I see many new supervisors make—it's the 80/20 rule again. Most supervisors spend 80 percent of their time coaching 20 percent of their employees—the ones who cause them problems. And they spend some time with the star employees because they like them and give them the most interesting work to do. But that group in the middle, your typical employees— 60 percent of your average workforce—gets no coaching. They don't cause trouble, and they don't shine. They just disappear into the woodwork and go unnoticed. Then it's time to do a performance appraisal, and you realize you don't know this person and have hardly said more than "good morning" since the last performance appraisal.

The coach's job is to coach all of the team members, not just the stars and the ones having trouble. After all, my future stars and potential problems are hovering in that middle group. Coaching takes place as a result of assigning work, setting goals, monitoring progress, training, and preparing for performance appraisals.

This is something I learned about coaching and giving feedback to employees: If you wait until they fail and tell them how to improve, you're criticizing them. It is after the fact and generally not appreciated. If you tell them before, with the intent to improve their performances and prevent failure, you're coaching. Here's another thing I've learned about coaching that's part of active listening and giving feedback: Coaches ask questions. It sounds like this:

- How else might you do that?
- What else have you tried?
- Have you thought of . . . ?
- What would happen if you did . . . ?

The whole idea is to help employees find their own answers and solutions. Leading questions can help them solve their own problems. There are certain times I know coaching will be needed, like with new employees; they need frequent coaching to get them started.

There are also other times when coaching is needed. One example is when you have a change in policy or procedures. Some employees make the transition quickly and easily, and others have a hard time with change and need to be coached through the process. It takes time, but it's important to get everyone on board, and it's one of my major responsibilities in developing my people.

Another time when heavy-duty coaching is needed is when there is a problem in behavior or performance, or preparing an employee to take on a new challenge. Let me show you how each of these examples applies to Chuck, Charleen, and Charles. Now that they've been here a while, I can see each needs coaching, but they need very different things from me. My challenge is to adjust my coaching to meet their needs.

Chuck is developing into a star employee. My coaching with him is to encourage the good work, keep him challenged by giving him new accounts and goals, and come up with ways to reinforce his successes. My concern is that he will move on to greener pastures in another company, maybe to a competitor. With his current success under his belt, he will soon recognize his own strength and talents. I need to help him continue growing and developing; maybe I could move into a mentor role with him. Let's see how *Active Listening* might be used to challenge Chuck.

Reflect

Coach: Hi, Chuck. How are things going? Tell me about the Vector account.

Chuck: That account is going well; I've been developing a good rapport with the general manager, and they're ordering on schedule with a sightly higher volume. I think the GM really likes me; we went to lunch last week and found we both play golf.

Coach: Sounds like it's going well, and you're pretty satisfied with the account.

Probe

Coach: Have you asked to meet the managers in their other divisions? We've dealt with the local division for a while, but I read that they're expanding overseas.

Chuck: No, but that gives me an idea; they're having a management seminar in a couple of months. I wonder if there's some way I can leverage on this and meet several other managers from other divisions.

Summarize

Coach: So you're going to arrange a golf game and find a way to meet the other managers. That would be a real advance with some fantastic possibilities for the company and for you. I'll be eager to hear what develops. Chuck, you're doing a great job. Let me know if you need my help or just want to bounce some ideas off me.

The objective is for me to encourage Chuck, let him know we appreciate him, and offer help if it is needed. Active listening is also effective when an employee comes to you with a problem and needs coaching to help work it out. For Chuck, it provides a sounding board for his ideas.

Charleen just does her job each day. No problems, no complaints. She is someone who is easily overlooked in the day-to-day hassle of fighting fires. Yet she, more than anyone, appreciates the one-on-one attention that coaching provides, and she could easily be motivated to produce more. I need to discover her strengths and talents so she can build on them and we can get the best from her. I need to motivate her by providing more interesting work when she's ready, perhaps giving her more autonomy. She likes to be in on things, so letting her know about planned changes in advance makes her feel more secure when the changes occur. Charleen is part of the group that could blossom with good coaching or disappear through neglect. Let's see how the *Feedback Cycle* might be used to motivate Charleen.

State the situation: Charleen, I understand from your supervisor that you're doing well with your job, but you're not learning new things. You said you're getting bored with counting inventory and need something more interesting. Now that you're more familiar with the organization, I wonder if you're ready to learn a new computer program for tracking shipments.

State your feelings: I believe you have a lot of potential that is not being used, and I'd like to talk with you about your work. You're young, and if you intend to grow with the company, you must become familiar with the new technology. We're moving in that direction, and I'd like to see you move with it.

Consequences: The result of your not taking the risk and becoming familiar with computers is that your current job will eventually become outdated, and you will be out of work. If you learn the new way of doing inventory and shipping, you will be prepared for our changes.

Results: I'd like to see you be more productive, take a few classes on your own to develop your computer skills. I'd also like you to operate this new shipping and tracking program by June.

The objective is to encourage and motivate Charleen. She has potential but needs a little push in the right direction.

Coaching Skills

Active Listening

- **Reflect**

  Listen to your employee and reflect back empathy and understanding of the situation.

- **Probe**

  Probe with questions to get more information and clarity and to help the employee see the situation more clearly.

- **Summarize**

  Repeat or paraphrase what you've heard to make sure you understand and to give the employee a chance to correct misunderstandings.

Giving Feedback

- State the situation.
- Describe how you feel about it.
- Tell them the consequences:
  - How their behavior affects others
  - What will happen if it continues
- Let them know what you want to happen.

(You can use this for both positive and corrective feedback.)

Charles has developed into a problem and needs lots of coaching. He has become part of the 20 percent who uses too much of my time to keep him on track and out of trouble. He just doesn't get along with other employees. They complain about his arrogant attitude and won't work with him. Since his job requires working with other departments and managers, he's not getting the job done. He does and says things that offend other employees. Because I respect his analytical ability and need his computer skills, I'm always covering for him. I really must do some problem solving with him. The biggest challenge will be to get Charles to admit—or just to see— that there is a problem. He tends to think it's everyone else's problem, not his.

For my coaching to have an impact, Charles will have to come up with his own solutions. I'll provide support and encouragement. This is a particularly difficult problem to address with an employee, because it's about attitude rather than performance. These *Problem-Solving Steps* might work with Charles.

Get agreement that a problem exists: Charles needs first to understand how a successful employee would work in his position. He needs to see the gap in order to acknowledge that there's a problem. His attitude has made him unproductive because the other managers won't work with him. He thinks they are all dinosaurs because they don't have his technical skills, and his attitude offends them. He needs to admit his feelings and change his behavior. He is rude, disrespectful, egotistical.

Discuss alternative solutions:
- Computer-skills class for all the managers
- Interpersonal skills training for Charles
- Working directly for different managers to understand their problems
- Team building for Charles and those he needs to work with
- 360° feedback could help

Agree on a plan of action: We decided to assign Charles to different units to work more closely with managers and understand their skills and abilities as well as their problems.

Follow up to evaluate progress and address barriers: Charles and I will meet weekly to see how his plan is going. He will have new performance goals and must get managers to work with him to succeed.

Recognize success or try another solution: Assigning Charles to different units did not work. His first two managers asked to have him taken out of their departments because he was disrupting the rapport in those units. We need to try another solution.

Even though Charles is difficult, I want to do all I can to help him out. After all, I made the decision to hire him. So now I'll try something else—a new action plan. I need to show him how to stop creating barriers for himself. If I could help him change his attitude, we could increase production, and he'd be more satisfied. Needless to say, those he works with would be happier, too. I'll try anything at this point to help Charles solve this problem.

Problem-Solving Steps

- Be sure the employee understands what is expected and sees the gap in his performance or behavior. Get agreement from the employee that a problem exists—this is half the battle. The employee needs to state the problem in his own words, not just nod in agreement.

- Mutually discuss alternative solutions. Get the employee to contribute to the list. The intent is to imply that there are many solutions, and together you will find one that works.

- Agree on a course of action.

- Follow-up to evaluate progress and to address barriers. An employee often runs into barriers beyond his or her control. Sometimes the coach can help.

- Recognize and reward success or try another solution.

Summary—Coaching Charlie
Key Points

- Coaching is a daily event .

- Spend time coaching your average employees: with proper motivation, they could become stars—with neglect, they could become problems.

- Criticism comes after someone fails; coaching happens before.

- Coaches ask lots of questions to help employees find their own answers.

- Listen to your employees; they might have good ideas.

- Give employees candid feedback when an event occurs.

- Getting employees to recognize their problem is half the battle.

- Yogi Berra *might* have said, "Your employees will know what you think . . . if you tell them."

Chapter 5

Performance Appraisals

- Why Do Them?

- Setting Goals and Career Planning

- Rewards and Reinforcements

- Disciplinary Process

Performance Appraisals—Why Do Them?

Performance appraisals—I hate them. Well, at least I used to hate them until I realized they can be a key tool to help my employees grow and develop. The yearly formal appraisal starts the ongoing process of setting goals and continuous coaching, which keeps us on track. The appraisal is revisited frequently as changes occur for the company and the employee. At the end of the year, it simply documents what occurred last year and what will happen next year.

Performance appraisals are used for setting goals, motivating employees, planning careers, rewarding and reinforcing success, identifying problems, and finally for termination.

Take Charleen, for example. Frankly, the time slips by and if I don't do a formal appraisal with her once a year, I might not spend a whole hour nose to nose, eye to eye, finding out about her and how she's doing. And I can't depend on her supervisor finding time either. We all seem to get caught up spending time with our problem people and dealing with daily crises.

Charleen comes in, does her job, and that's it. The formal, yearly appraisal makes me and her supervisor take time to look at her file, review her goals, and talk with her. She is doing fine, and frankly, she wants to hear it from me—affirmation or reassurance that she is okay.

Actually, she is quite a person: a young mother taking care of two kids on her own. I'm proud of her, and I need to tell her so now and then. She's doing a good job here and gets on well with her coworkers.

Setting Goals and Career Planning

For Charleen, I use the performance appraisal to clarify goals, motivate her to continue to grow, suggest training, identify which of her skills we can use, and find out what support she needs from me. I've read some surprising studies about motivating employees. I used to think that money and promotions were the only important things to employees. They were not the most important to me, but I thought they were the most important to my employees. Then I read a study by Kenneth Kovach of George Mason University: It showed that what employees really want is appreciation and interesting work. Well, that's certainly true of Charleen, and as her manager, I can provide both of those. When it comes to motivation, a manager's or supervisor's assumptions can often be wrong.

You need to consider the individuals. Ask them what motivates them, and you might get some surprises. At first, they'll say money, but a little probing will uncover the other important motivators. So what I've learned about performance appraisals is that they can motivate my employees if they're used well.

What Motivates Employees

1. Interesting work

2. Appreciation of work done

3. Being "in on things"

4. Job security

5. Good wages

6. Promotions

7. Good working conditions

8. Personal loyalty to employees

9. Tactful discipline

10. Sympathetic help with personal problems

Study by Kenneth Kovach, George Mason University, 1995

Our company used to link appraisals directly to salary. We had an operations-development consultant come in a while ago, and we revised the system and the forms. Seems like a pendulum that keeps swinging, looking for the perfect system, which we haven't found yet. We never have had a performance-appraisal system everyone liked. Searching for the perfect one is like searching for the Holy Grail.

All performance appraisals have these things in common:

- Some forms to provide consistency throughout the company

- At least one annual face-to-face meeting with my employees

- Required documents, records, files, and data to provide justification for comments, decisions, suggestions

- An opportunity for communication: coaching, counseling, feedback to improve performance

I think back to when I was an employee. I hardly ever saw my boss and always wondered if he knew me well enough to appraise my performance. It was a lot more important to me than it seemed to him. My boss was always very busy, and any time he spent with me seemed like a gift.

Here's how we do it now. To begin with, the employee gets forms to fill out with goals, accomplishments, and ratings on how they think they did. At the same time, I fill out a few forms regarding their progress. Then we meet, discuss what each of us wrote, and agree on what the employee accomplished since last year and what needs to be achieved this year. We agree on any necessary monthly or quarterly follow-up. Then I submit the forms to Human Resources for review and filing. I get copies, the employee gets copies—it usually goes quite well. I've learned that the more coaching and feedback I give to employees during the year, the smoother the performance appraisal goes. You know the old saying, "no surprises."

As often as I've done this, I still have a few questions. For example, I know appraisals are supposed to stick to business, focus on the job and goals; but how do I get to know employees without talking about their interests, hobbies, family, and other personal things? Also, if we don't agree, should I change my appraisal, or will that cause all employees to overrate themselves? And I have questions about the system this organization is currently using. Is it better to link salary to the performance appraisal or keep it separate? Should we use standard forms for every job, or be able to tailor them? How much should this be based on numbers? Do we really have to quantify our appraisals? Well, I don't make these decisions. I just use the current system.

Here's another thing I wonder about: How much of my employees' performance is based on my management skills and style? Would their appraisals be better if I'd paid more attention to their progress? And would another manager rate an employee the same as I did, or are my personal feelings about my employees skewing their appraisals? I've tried to be a decent role model and make my expectations very clear. I've tried to provide the resources and support they need and be candid and accurate with my appraisals. Still, I have these questions after my many years of experience. Performance appraisal is one of my primary tools for helping employees grow and develop. Yet, every performance-appraisal system I've used leaves some unanswered questions. It's not easy to grow great employees, and it's not easy to be a great manager.

Performance Appraisal

1. **Preparing for the Interview**

    Review the employee's last appraisal. Determine strengths as well as weaknesses to be discussed (have specific observations and documentation). Consider what development or change is needed. Give the employee enough time to do his or her own preparation.

2. **Conducting the Interview**
    - Set a conducive environment.
    - Clarify that this is a two-way discussion for mutual problem solving and goal setting.
    - Talk about job performance.
    - Let the employee talk first (observations, perceptions of problems, goals, etc.).
    - Agree on joint objectives.
    - Summarize and agree on follow-up.

3. **Post-interview Activity**
    - Document the discussion and the agreement (cc the employee).
    - Follow up on commitments you made.
    - Evaluate results—How did it go? What could you do better next time?

Adapted from *Performance Appraisal in the Public Sector* by George Morrisey

Rewards and Reinforcements

What a pleasure to prepare for an appraisal with Chuck. Who doesn't enjoy telling someone how well he's doing and that you are proud of him? All I need is a few minutes to review his file and his accomplishments; he has certainly lived up to my expectations.

Now I need to focus on ways to develop his future here and reward him for his success. I want to encourage him to see career opportunities within our organization. This is one employee I don't want our competitors to find. I need to find out which work he considers interesting and challenging, and how much independence he can handle. Then I'll help him focus on long-term goals. He has a tendency to be shortsighted and not plan far enough ahead. He gets so busy doing what he does that he doesn't focus on developing his skills and increasing his knowledge.

There should be some tangible reward attached to such an outstanding appraisal. Since pay-for-performance is not part of our system, I need to be creative in finding ways to encourage Chuck and reinforce his good work.

First thing I'll do is walk through the Career Development Plan to reinforce the idea of his future with us. I wonder if he knows the company will help him acquire a higher degree. I wonder if he thought of being a presenter at our annual conference. That would give him some recognition, a way to consider what makes him successful, and a way to share it with others. I've received several calls and letters from customers saying how much they enjoy working with him. This hasn't happened in the past.

There are a few key ideas when it comes to considering rewards for employees. The first: Rewards must be considered rewarding to those who receive them. One organization I know rewarded employees by treating them to dinner with their boss. Maybe the boss thought it was rewarding. The employees did not. I find out what my employees consider rewarding and build our reward system around their suggestions. I am repeatedly surprised to find they don't ask for the stars: They ask for pizza parties and celebrations, because it's not about pizza, it's about recognition and appreciation.

Another key is to reward appropriately. A huge accomplishment deserves a huge reward. If the same reward, like a plaque or certificate, is given for everything, then the reward loses its value.

Career Development Plan

1. Identify important factors

_____ challenging work

_____ responsibility

_____ autonomy

_____ advancement

_____ pay

_____ status

_____ (other factors)

2. Identify goals

one year =

five years =

3. Identify skills, knowledge, attitudes needed

skills:

knowledge:

attitudes:

4. Interventions to acquire experience

5. Reality check

Are career objectives realistic?

6. Develop an action plan to achieve goals

-
-

Another key has to do with company values. The reward system must reinforce your company values. Sometimes it can backfire, like when a major company rewarded auto technicians for selling new parts, and the technicians started replacing good parts to earn the reward. A call center rewarded employees for the number of calls they completed, which encouraged agents to be curt instead of courteous and helpful.

The last key is that a reward must be available to everyone. I have seen dissension among employees when one division in a public utility gave employees time off as a reward, and other divisions were not allowed to do so. I need to think about which rewards are appropriate and available to my employees, and which will be meaningful to them. Boy, I'm looking forward to doing an appraisal for Chuck; it will be mostly "praise-all."

Incentives and Rewards

- Incentives are offered before the job.
- Rewards are given after the job.

  KEY—Rewards must be rewarding to those who receive them.

  KEY—Rewards and incentives must be appropriate, based on achievements.

  KEY—Rewards and incentives must be available to everyone.

  KEY—Rewards must reinforce the organization's goals.

Ideas

- Money
- Time off
- Favorite work
- Awards, prizes, certificates, plaques
- Personal development— classes, conference
- Choice of schedule and overtime
- Letters of praise
- Improved office environment
- Participation in customer visits

- Promotions
- Special assignments
- Autonomy over work
- Fun—parties, celebrations
- Greater visibility to upper management
- Ability to travel
- Public recognition— newsletters, ceremonies
- Gifts—dinner for two, trips, tickets to events
- Others

Disciplinary Process

I have to do an appraisal with Charles, and this one won't be easy. We'll use the appraisal to start disciplinary action that might lead to termination. He has received several verbal warnings through our frequent coaching and problem-solving sessions. Last week, I gave him a formal verbal warning. I described the situation as I saw it and told him what the consequences would be.

It's never easy to terminate a permanent employee. Once an employee has passed his or her initial probationary period, you can no longer say to that person, "Sorry, this isn't going to work out." Instead, you must carefully follow your organization's disciplinary process. This usually includes several steps: verbal warnings, written warnings, time to improve, another written warning . . . and it goes on and on. It takes a long, long time.

Today, we have our performance appraisal interview, and my forms are marked with an overall "unsatisfactory." I've documented how we've tried to turn things around. I'll also include a written warning on our official company form.

Sometimes, when managers write an unsatisfactory appraisal, the disgruntled employee argues, yells, cries . . . or worse. If you've been coaching and problem solving with the employee, the "unsatisfactory" should be no surprise for that person. Nevertheless, some employees refuse to recognize or admit to an "unsatisfactory."

If things get out of hand or an employee reacts in a way that catches me off guard, I will reschedule the meeting. This gives me time to figure out how to handle the situation. There was an occasion when I listened to the employee and decided that my appraisal was too harsh. I felt guilty for not doing my homework, and I didn't have solid examples of the problem.

Remember, an appraisal must be able to stand up in court—with the judge taking the employee's side. I must be able to prove this person deserves to be terminated. A couple of years ago, written appraisals actually served me well. I was finally able to fire this guy after months of his declining performance and his poor attitude. After all the rigor involved in disciplinary action, the turkey sued me. He took the company—and me, personally—to court for unfair dismissal. He brought up everything under the sun: discrimination, favoritism, stress, everything. Fortunately, I had records of his past five performance appraisals and notes from various coaching sessions, all of which were considered legal documentation in court. So we were able to defend terminating him. At that point, I understood one of the key reasons why we do performance appraisals regularly.

Most of the time, I take the performance-appraisal process as an opportunity to develop my employees. I do my homework because I realize that although I do lots of these, employees only get one, and it's very important to them—to their self-esteem and career development.

If an employee doesn't agree with my appraisal, he or she always has the right to appeal to my boss, who reviews all of the appraisals I do. Sometimes the employee won't sign the forms, even after I explain that a signature means they were appraised, not that they agree with the appraisal. Our current forms have a place for employee comments, and some employees write an attachment to describe their point of view when they disagree with the appraisal.

There are some who want to take their issue to a higher authority, and that's okay too. Most of the time, HR and my boss will back me up because I have plenty of documentation. Termination is a last resort. It's time consuming and painful for everyone—like a divorce. That's why many supervisors will put up with problem employees and learn to cope rather than terminate them. Some managers play a trading game with problem employees: "I'll take yours if you take mine."

Developing employees and ending the year writing outstanding appraisals are the best part of being a supervisor. Trying to develop employees and ending the year writing unsatisfactory appraisals and taking disciplinary action are the worst parts.

One last word: Don't be Mr. Nice Guy; it creates mediocrity. Be candid and be fair.

Steps for Disciplinary Action

Action Taken	Documentation
Verbal warning	Memo to the employee
Meeting on verbal warning	Discuss with manager
Written warning	Official form—copies to: • Employee • Human Resources Department file
Follow up on required actions	Discuss with HR and the manager
Remove warning or issue second written warning	Official form—copies to: • Employee • Human Resources Department file
Termination meeting	HR and manager

Adapted from Robert Bramson, Problem Behavior Course #C17Ill-7

Summary—Performance Appraisals
Key Points

- Performance appraisals are a key tool for growing great employees.

- Be considerate—managers do many, but employees receive only one.

- Performance appraisals give you an opportunity to pat some backs.

- Performance appraisals provide an opportunity for career planning and goal setting.

- Don't encourage mediocrity by overrating employees.

- There should be no surprises at performance-appraisal time.

- Performance appraisals summarize all of your employee development efforts:

    - Hiring and orientation
    - Assigning work and setting goals
    - Training employees
    - Coaching and problem solving
    - Terminating and promoting

Chapter 6
Looking Back

- Could Have—
  Should Have

- Probation

Looking Back
Could Have—Should Have

Looking back over the past two years at my three Charlies, I wonder if I did as much as I could have to help them grow and be successful. I have several years of experience under my belt, but I still try to keep up with recent management theory and what's going on in other organizations. I read my association journals, take a seminar now and then, and read some new books. Now I wonder if I could have done more. Looking back, there are some things I did right and some things I could have done better.

Here's an example of something that worked. A while back, one of our best customers merged with another company and changed a lot of the ways they do business. So I pulled together all of our people who do business with this customer, and we met with the customer to figure out how to work with its new managers. All three of my Charlies were in this group, as well as the customer. Later, I read we'd created a "cross-functional process-action team" that's part of total quality management.

Here's another example of something I read about in a management journal that worked well. I took each of my Charlies to lunch and asked them to tell me about the changes they would make in their department, if they were me. Sometimes it's hard to see things from the employees' point of view, so I thought I would ask them. It served my original purpose of getting some good ideas, and it served another, unintended purpose—I realized there are some things employees are required to do that they don't fully understand. This gave me an opportunity to explain why some things are done the way they are. Once the employees understood the impact on other departments, or the total sequence of events, they were willing to do the task with a new and improved attitude.

I could have done some things better. Charles might have changed if I had been more participative with him. I honestly tried everything I could think of because I considered him a challenge and respected his technical skills. But technical skills aren't enough to succeed here. People aren't always fired because they cannot do the work; often it's because they can't get along. When others won't work with them, they are unable to do their jobs.

When it became apparent Charles wasn't working out well, I tried putting him on an established work team, hoping the organizational culture would rub off on him from other employees.

The team decided Charles was disruptive and asked that he attend their meetings only as a guest when specific computer skills were an issue. The facilitator said Charles was patronizing and talked down to others who weren't as well educated as he.

I tried sending him to a seminar on interpersonal skills so he could see how others operate and learn how to view things from their perspective. It helped him understand his uniqueness in this organization, but it backfired and added to his discontent.

I tried matching him with various managers as a special assistant to understand their needs and help with their technology problems. The managers claimed his suggestions were so foreign to the way they operated that the changes he recommended were impractical and too costly.

I tried frequent coaching sessions, but that didn't work either. He had an attitude that all of us here are pretty stupid, that this company is something from the Dark Ages, and that only he can see the light. The worst part is he makes no attempt to hide these feelings. We may not be as cutting edge as some organizations, but we are successful and have been in business for a long time. Someone does *something* right around here.

Looking back, I should have cut the strings during Charles' initial probationary period. I had an inclination from the start, but I thought I could do magic. There were clear indicators that although Charles had the technical skills we needed, his personality was not going to work out here.

Charles belongs in one of those small, high-tech organizations with others like him or, better yet, as his own boss. I bet other managers look back on the probationary period of other employees who didn't work out well and recognize indicators they should have acted on. It is so difficult to spend time and energy hiring, training, coaching, and developing employees just to terminate them in the end. Oh well . . . we do the best we can.

I'm proud to look back at Chuck and his progress here. I can't take too much credit; Chuck was a winner from the start. I had a good feeling about him and the job he would do for us. Chuck, the job, and our company culture were a good match. I gave him enough autonomy to do his job and was there to coach him when he needed it. I challenged him to think about the future and plan his career and his personal development.

With companies being downsized, rightsized, or whatever they call it now, there are fewer managers and supervisors around to micromanage. We must train people and empower them, whether we want to or not. However, empowerment is tricky. Take Chuck, for example. He's out in the field, and I'm not there to look over his shoulder. He has to be empowered to make decisions for his customers. It's my job to teach him what I know about good and bad decisions and teach him again when he screws up. Then I have no choice but to get out of his way and let him do his job. When he comes to me for advice, I'll be there.

Chuck has grown and flourished here beyond my expectations. Last month, he was given the Employee-of-the-Year Award. I'm very proud of him.

I'm even more proud of the progress made by Charleen. Only two years ago, this was her first job, and she was scared to death. She had no self-confidence and no plans for the future—all she wanted was a job. Now she has learned to do all of the tasks in the mail room, including operating the computer. She has made sensible suggestions for improving our process and has proved to be a dependable employee with plenty of common sense. She even looks more mature and self-assured. I believe I helped motivate and influence Charleen. She often dropped by my office to ask for my advice and opinion. My coaching techniques seemed to pay off in this case. Charleen is ready to continue to grow and develop.

Looking back, I'd have to say that management is quite a challenge, and the development of my employees is an awesome responsibility. Yet, if I expect to meet my department goals, I need people who can grow—with some nurturing from me—so we can stay productive and competitive in today's environment.

Summary—Looking Back
Key Points

- Occasional reflection can help you learn from your mistakes and celebrate your successes.

- Every story is not a success story.

- Pay more attention to your intuition.

- It is easier to cut your losses during an employee's initial probationary period than waiting to terminate.

- Management is difficult because every employee is unique.

- If in doubt—do the right thing!

Chapter 7

Good-Bye, Charlie

- Termination
- Promotions and Transfers

Good-Bye, Charlie

It's been three years since I hired Chuck, Charleen, and Charles. Today I lost the last one from my employment. As a manager or supervisor, I've seen many employees pass through my life. Some I really like and get very attached to, some I never get to know very well, and some become a pain in the neck. But they are all mine, and I'm responsible for their development.

While they're with me, I need to manage their performance to the best of my ability for two reasons. First, their growth and development means improved performance and increased productivity. That helps me succeed. Second, their futures, in part, depend on my guidance, encouragement, expectations, and support. They know I expect a lot and that I'm here to coach them, provide resources, and do whatever I can to unlock their potential. This makes them happy and promotes a good attitude about me and the organization.

It doesn't mean they stay here forever. That's not what I want, and it's not in their best interests. I'm proud of my reputation as a boss who "launders" employees. I get them, clean them up, train them . . . and out they go. This may take several years, but I see myself as a mentor—someone who helps employees grow, develop, and move on.

Termination

The first to go was Charles. I keep asking myself if I did everything possible with this kid. I coached him, sent him to classes, put him on a team that worked well together hoping some of its good vibes would rub off on him. I gave him a couple of good books to read, but he only wanted to read computer magazines. He started spending more and more time on the Internet—doing research, he said—and less time doing the work I hired him to do. Also, there was this ego thing. He thought he knew so much, and he did know a lot about computers, but he didn't know anything about getting along with other people, working with a team, and toning down his "I'm-better-than-you" attitude.

So, I had to go through all the steps in our disciplinary procedure. We have a 90-day probationary period in this organization. I sensed the problem from the beginning and kept thinking I could handle it. Problem is, it wasn't just me he had to get along with—there were others who had to handle him and his ego, and they couldn't deal with him. Looking back, it would have saved us all a lot of grief if I had gotten rid of him during probation. No obligation then; just say it isn't working out and cut the string.

Progressive discipline is a real pain. First, you have to ask yourself some serious questions that might be asked if you find yourself in court over wrongful termination. Questions like:

- Do performance appraisals support this action? (You can't give a satisfactory appraisal and then fire someone for poor performance.)

- Did I coach the employee and give him or her every opportunity to improve?

- Was the employee given fair warning that his or her behavior would cause termination?

I believe I did all those things with Charles. Fact is, it's hard to measure this kind of problem and support it on performance issues. It finally came down to his inability to do his job because the rest of the workforce wouldn't cooperate with him. Since I can't fire the whole workforce, I had to fire Charles. First I gave him proper verbal warnings in numerous coaching sessions. Next I gave him an official verbal warning that would lead to progressive discipline. I then issued a written warning on the official disciplinary form. This went into my file, a copy went to Human Resources, and a copy went to Charles. I hoped this would shake him up enough to make some serious changes. I gave him assignments and production goals. But he just couldn't make it happen. I gave him another written warning. Our company is pretty lenient: We give two verbal and two written warnings. There was no surprise when it came time to terminate.

This last meeting is the hardest part of my job. I never know what kind of reaction to expect from an employee, so I always have the HR manager with me. She seems to know how to handle those emotional situations. The key element in terminating an employee is documentation. Charles actually denied certain events occurred and said some conversations never took place. Fortunately, I documented every coaching session we had regarding his problem attitude and behavior. I had only sparse notes here and there, but they recapped what occurred, and I had dated them. They were all I needed to validate my case.

When it finally happened, I was sure there was no hope for Charles at this company. We had our last discussion with HR in Charles' office. Lucky thing, too, because he was so upset we had to leave and take a short break while he composed himself. It would have been difficult to leave him in my office. We held this meeting on a Friday afternoon, after everyone else left work. That meant Charles would not have to face the other employees and would have the weekend to think about his next steps. The HR person gave him some ideas on other jobs and assured him she wouldn't give him bad references should other companies call. The HR person had his last paycheck in hand and a list of items to recover: keys, files, manuals, and a few other things. At one point, the HR person gave Charles the option of resigning instead of being terminated. He decided to take that option.

Good-bye, Charles.

Promotions and Transfers

The next person I lost was Chuck. This was a pleasure and a feather in my cap. He proved to be everything I hoped for— and more. He stopped being my employee when he was promoted to a regional position. We are all hoping he can create some clones out there. I can't take too much credit; he was a star from the start. He gives me credit for helping him get organized, for understanding the importance of follow-through, and for having great expectations of him. These are the guys you hate to lose—although he is not a loss. He still works for us and we'll stay in touch. He simply is not my employee any longer.

Good-bye, Chuck.

Today I lost Charleen. She still works here, but she transferred to another department. She has been a good, steady worker all of these years and has matured well. As her kids got older and more independent, she started taking classes at night at the local community college to get a degree in communications. It's a shame more employees don't take advantage of our educational reimbursement program. Charleen did, and grew out of her position in the mail room.

Her termination from my employment amounted to a lateral transfer. There was no way for her to progress in her current position, so she needed a lateral move. Routine work was fine for her when she started here. That was three years ago, and she has come a long way. I heard about an administrative assistant position opening up for one of the vice presidents. His assistant is going to retire. I spoke to Charleen about it, and she was delighted. I then talked to the vice president and arranged for him to meet Charleen informally. He liked her; I knew he would. The transfer arrangements were made, and she starts her new job today.

Good-bye, Charleen.

So I've lost all three of my Charlies. One was promoted, one transferred, and one fired. As a manager, you can't hold your people captive; you need to process them through your operation. You're training good people to become your peers. Your job is to lose people, not keep them. We are in a hiring freeze again. It will end when the economy improves. When it ends, I get a new group of employees who will pass through my department; be under my care and supervision for a while; and benefit from my mentoring, coaching, and discipline. And so, it will be my job to grow more great employees.

Summary—Good-Bye Charlie
Key Points

- As a manager, employees pass through your life, and it's your job to develop them from "hello to good-bye."

- There are three ways to say good-bye:
  - "You're fired."
  - "You're transferred."
  - "You're promoted."

- Terminating an employee is very difficult: It's like a divorce—it takes a long time and lots of paper.

- An alternative to termination is to trade your problem employee for someone else's problem employee.

- Happy, productive managers make happy, productive employees . . . or is it happy, productive employees make happy, productive managers?

Note from the Author

Jane Holcomb, Ph.D.
7805 W. 80th Street
Playa del Rey, CA 90293
Phone # 310/821-7624
FAX # 310/821-0507

❐ Seminars, Workshops, Presentations

❐ Additional Books; Bulk Rates

❐ Customized Training

❐ *Make Training Worth Every Penny:*

    ❐ Book—$20.00

    ❐ Video—$200.00